DJING

John Steventon
(Recess)

CLASH
by ticktock

T781.49

Copyright © ticktock Entertainment Ltd 2009

First published in Great Britain in 2009 by ticktock Media Ltd,
The Old Sawmill, 103 Goods Station Road, Tunbridge Wells, Kent, TN1 2DP

project editor and picture researcher: Ruth Owen
ticktock project designer: Simon Fenn

Thank you to Lorraine Petersen and the members of nasen

ISBN 978 1 84696 937 9 pbk

Printed in China

Picture credits (t=top; b=bottom; c=centre; l=left; r=right):
age fotostock/SuperStock: 18. Creative Commons Attribution ShareAlike (Wikipedia): 11b.
Film Magic/Getty Images: 9, 16-17. Shutterstock: OFC, 1, 2-3, 4-5, 6-7 (background), 6, 7t, 7b, 8, 10, 12-13
(background), 13b, 18-19 (background), 19, 20, 21, 25, 28-29, 31. John Steventon: 14-15, 24t, 24b. Tetra
Images/SuperStock: 26-27. Ticktock Media Archive: 11t, 12, 13t, 16t, 22-23.

CONTENTS

‘ **The air in the club is hot.**

ere's a smell of aftershave, perfume and y ice in the air.

e music is so loud the floor is shaking.

e lights are flashing...

...and I've just put on a song that has made a thousand people cheer, put their hands in the air and dance.

You've got to love it
when that happens! "

Recess

Chapter 2

WHAT IS A DJ?

What makes a DJ different from someone who just plays a CD, ejects it, puts in another one and then hits play?

The difference is that DJs have two turntables or CD players. This allows them to "mix" from song to song. So the music plays non-stop all night.

Turntables

Francis Grasso was a DJ in New York City in the 1970s. Grasso invented two important techniques for the dance DJ.

SLIPCUEING

Slipcueing is when the DJ holds a record still at an exact point, such as a bass drumbeat. The turntable's platter turns underneath.

Platter

The DJ then starts the record at the exact same time as the bass drumbeat from the song that's finishing. The DJ doesn't have to wait for the turntable to get up to full speed.

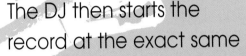

BEATMATCHING

As one song finishes, the speed of the next song has already been matched to it. This means the people on the dance floor don't have to speed up or slow down their dancing.

From the discos of the 1970s, to the huge nightclubs of Ibiza, Grasso's techniques are still in use.

A DJ's job is to play great music. It's also the DJ's job to make the music sound great.

Practising your techniques and having the right equipment will make the music sound great.

But what is great music?

What you might think is a great record, someone else might use to put their coffee cup on.

When you are a DJ, it's important to remember it's not just about what YOU think!

You must play the music that the people on the dance floor want to hear. If you do, you will give them the best night of their lives.

Then you're a great DJ.

> *Thousands of fans pack stadiums to listen to superstar DJ Tiesto. They love how he mixes the biggest trance anthems.*

Chapter 3

EQUIPMENT

So what do you need to be a DJ apart from lots of music?

If you are playing records, you will need turntables. If you are playing CDs, you will need CD players. DJs call these "decks".

DJ decks are different from home CD players and record players. They have a part called a pitch control.

The pitch control allows a DJ to change the speed of the music when beatmatching.

CD player

Pitch control

Record player

DJ decks must also be able to play the music without it skipping or jumping. Even if it's so loud the walls are shaking!

To change the music from one deck to another, the DJ uses a "mixer".

Each deck plugs into an input channel on the mixer.

Basic mixers have two channels, so you can use two decks. Each channel has a volume control, usually a vertical slider.

Two channel mixer

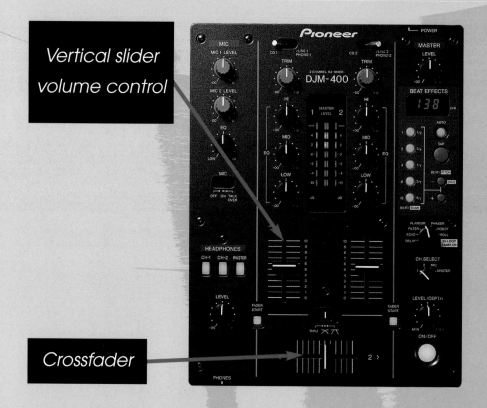

Vertical slider volume control

Crossfader

The mixer also has another slider control which goes from side to side. This is called a crossfader. It makes the music from one deck quieter as the other one gets louder.

Professional DJ mixers have a lot more controls on them. They can also have a lot more input channels.

DJs can use these mixers to change the sound of the music. The DJ can add effects, such as an echo.

Six channel mixer

The DJ can even record a short section of the music and play it over and over again. This is called playing a "sample".

Many DJs are now adding computers to their DJ set-ups.

They can use software such as *Traktor Scratch* or *Serato Live*.

This software allows the DJ to use their decks and mixer to mix songs playing from the computer's hard drive!

Record deck

Mixer

DJ software

CD deck

The people on the dance floor need to hear the music you're playing! So, you will need an amplifier and some very loud speakers.

Amplifier

Headphones

Chapter 4

MUSIC

If you're DJing in a nightclub, the kind of music you will play will depend on the club. If you try to play rock at a trance club, you'll probably be asked to leave very quickly!

As a nightclub DJ, you will often play music that is in the charts or is popular at that moment.

To find out what's popular:
- Read reviews of new music in magazines and on websites.
- Listen to specialist radio shows.
- Look at DJ charts.

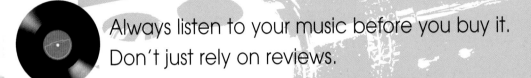

TIPS ON BUYING MUSIC

Always listen to your music before you buy it. Don't just rely on reviews.

If you're DJing at parties, buy compilation albums. Compilation albums will have lots of the songs you'll need on one album.

Beatport and *iTunes* can save you money. You will only need to buy the song or remix you want, not the whole album.

Check records are not scratched or dirty.

It's harder to know what music to play if you're DJing at a birthday party or a wedding.

The guests at a party will like many different kinds of music.

Try to get invited to lots of parties. Listen to what the DJs play, and watch how the crowd reacts.

" When you are DJing at a wedding, check who is on the dance floor. This is your guide to the best music to play. If grandma and grandpa are on the dance floor, you might not want to play gangsta rap! "

Recess

As the DJ at a wedding or party, you may have to speak to the crowd using a microphone.

Microphone

You might need to say what the next song is. Or you might need to tell everyone that the food is ready.

Turn down the volume control on the music and speak clearly and loudly.

Chapter 5

TECHNIQUES

So, you've picked the right music. Now you must make sure you change from song to song in the best possible way.

The crossfader makes the song you want to stop playing go quieter. This is called "fading out". It also makes the next song louder. This is called "fading in".

Assign controls

Crossfader

Mixers with more than two channels use assign controls.

These let the mixer know which input channel to fade out or fade in.

EQ – Equalisation controls

Vertical sliders

If one of the songs is too loud or too quiet, adjust the vertical slider for the correct channel.

One song may have more bass sounds than another, or the singing may be louder. The EQ (equalisation) controls on a mixer allow you to adjust this.

You can even add or remove sounds such as the bass drums.

BEATMATCHING

A bass drum beat plays through most dance music. The amount of times this beat plays in a minute is known as BPM (beats per minute).

BPM counter

A song might have a BPM of 132. But the next song has a BPM of 125.

The DJ will use the pitch control to speed up the second song to 132 BPM.

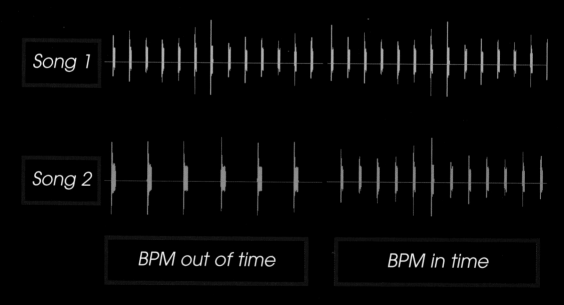

Song 1

Song 2

BPM out of time   BPM in time

This gives the music a constant beat for dancing.

SCRATCHING

A scratch DJ will play a song on one deck. Then the DJ will stop the song on the other deck with his or her hand.

The DJ uses their hand to play a very short part of the song backwards and forwards. They do this in time to the music playing from the other deck.

The speed and way that the DJ moves the record can turn a simple drumbeat or word into something that sounds great.

Chapter 6

GETTING NOTICED

One way to get noticed is to hold your own parties and DJ at them.

If you are good at what you do, people might ask you to DJ at their party.

Make a "demo mix" CD.
Pick the best music you
can, mix well and make
the mix sound great.

Record your mix onto CDs
and write your name and address
on them. Always carry your CDs
with you.

Chapter 7

MY FIRST NIGHT DJING

"

DJing is one of the coolest, most fun things I've done. But my first night DJing was a disaster.

I played music that I wanted to play – not the music the crowd wanted. The crowd wasn't happy and they didn't dance.

I stopped the wrong record by accident. Suddenly everything went silent. I thought the deck on the left had just stopped playing music. But it was the one on the right!

The headphones cable rubbed against my shirt buttons and undid most of them. I didn't realise until after I'd stopped playing that I'd been showing my bare chest to everyone! **"**

Recess

amplifier Music in the mixer is not very loud. An amplifier is a piece of equipment that makes the music louder before it is played out through the speakers.

bass The booming sounds from music, such as the bass drums or bass guitar.

crossfader A sliding control on the mixer. It changes the music sent out from the mixer from one input channel to the other.

DJ Short for "disc jockey". A person who plays records at a nightclub or at a party. Also, a person who plays music and hosts a radio show.

equalisation control (EQ) A control which allows a DJ to make sounds, such as drums or voices, louder or quieter.

input channel Where a deck plugs into a mixer.

mix To make one song quieter while, at the same time, making the next one louder.

mixer The piece of equipment a DJ uses to change from song to song.

pitch control The control on a deck which adjusts the speed of the music.

review A report in which someone gives an opinion about a piece of work, such as a record or a book.

technique A way of doing something.

trance A style of music played in nightclubs. It is very musical with a beat that's similar to a dancer's heartbeat. This puts the people on the dance floor into an energetic, happy mood.

volume control A control that makes the music louder or quieter.

When you are DJing:

- Take as many CDs, records or MP3s as you can – too many songs is better than not enough!

- Concentrate in the DJ booth. Think about what song has stopped, then take the needle off the record or eject the CD.

- Try to record everything you do so you can listen later, and improve your skills.

- Never forget your demo mix CD.

DJING ONLINE

Websites

http://www.recess.co.uk
Recess's (John Steventon) "how to DJ" website

www.djacademy.org.uk
A DJ academy

http://www.dmcworld.com/charts/
A website of DJ charts